2008
Survivor
June 6, 2008

Celebrate.

Remember.

Fight Back.

Survivor Committee
Brenda Z   Cherie N
Mike N, Kathy M.

LIFE'S LITTLE PLEASURES

a perfect day

LIFE'S LITTLE PLEASURES

a perfect day

RYLAND
PETERS
& SMALL
LONDON NEW YORK

Designer Luana Gobbo

Senior editor Henrietta Heald

Picture research Emily Westlake

Production Gemma Moules

Art director Gabriella Le Grazie

Publishing director Alison Starling

First published in the USA in 2005 by
Ryland Peters & Small, Inc.
519 Broadway
5th Floor
New York, NY 10012
www.rylandpeters.com
10 9 8 7 6 5 4 3 2 1

Library of Congress Cataloging-in-Publication Data

A perfect day : life's little pleasures.
    p. cm.
  ISBN 1-84172-980-9
  1. Home economics. 2. Cookery.
  TX147.P384 2005
  640--dc22

                                    2005002958

Printed and bound in China.

contents

*I*ntroduction

There are many things that go to make up the perfect day—and the choice will vary from person to person—but there are some small joys that almost all of us would agree on. These range from an invigorating shower before work, enlivened with a few drops of rosemary oil, to slipping between freshly ironed cotton sheets last thing at night, from the scent of lavender when you open a drawer to a mug of steaming hot chocolate on a cold day.

Celebrating the importance of life's little pleasures, *A Perfect Day* includes tempting recipes for snacks and drinks and a host of other ideas for indulging yourself. It shows that something as simple as finding the ideal pair of shoes in a sale or curling up on the sofa with a friend to watch your favorite film can make all the difference between a mundane day and one that is special and memorable.

*A*n *invigorating shower*

A revitalizing aromatic shower
is a matchless way to recharge your body and
your senses first thing in the morning. Sprinkle six
to eight drops of stimulating rosemary pure essential
oil in the shower tray, turn on the water, and step in.
Enjoy the burst of freshness that will invigorate
your body from top to toe.

*T*he first cup of coffee of the day

Making coffee in the proper way lets you appreciate to the full the fresh, rich flavors on offer. The principles described here make all the difference between aromatic energy and insipid meekness or brutish bitterness.

❀ Buy good-quality, freshly roasted whole beans and grind them just before brewing.

❀ The grind should be just right for whatever method you are using—finely ground for espresso, medium fine for filter coffee, and coarsely ground for a French press.

❀ Measure the amounts of coffee and water used and the length of time for brewing. Getting the right proportions and letting the coffee and water brew together for the correct length of time means you extract the most character and aromatic oils from the bean without the brew becoming bitter. For weaker coffee, it is preferable to add hot water to properly brewed coffee than to use too much water or too few beans.

❀ Pour the water onto the coffee grounds when it is just off the boil. This will dissolve the soluble flavors from the coffee without scalding the subtleties of the coffee taste into bitterness.

❀ Do not attempt to keep coffee warm on the heat—it will stew and become bitter.

A healthy breakfast that you know will do you good—and make you feel virtuous

After tasting this granola, you will forget all other granolas, as well as feeling satisfied at having made your own breakfast. Store the cereal in an airtight container for up to four weeks—if it lasts that long!

1½ cups (300 g) rolled oats
2 oz (50 g) whole almonds
2 oz (50 g) raisins
1 oz (25 g) ready-to-eat dried apricots
1 oz (25 g) pumpkin seeds
3 tablespoons (25 g) golden superfine
   sugar
4 tablespoons maple syrup

a non-stick baking sheet

serves 4

❀ Mix all the ingredients together in a large bowl, then transfer to the baking sheet.
❀ Bake in a preheated oven at 325°F (160°C) for 25 minutes until toasted.
❀ Remove from the oven and stir well.
❀ Return the mixture to the oven and cook for a further 15 minutes until the granola is crisp and light golden. Remove from the oven.
❀ Eat the cereal while hot with milk, or let cool, then transfer to an airtight container and store.

The scent of lavender when you open a drawer

To make your own lavender bags for scenting drawers, pick lavender in full bloom and hang it up for a couple of weeks in a warm, dry room before pulling the dried flowers off each stem. Or buy lavender mail order. Any scrap of fabric can be used to make a bag, but fine lawn or organza is especially good. Seal the bag with a piece of ribbon or lace and refill it with fresh lavender every year. Potpourri or dried rose petals also make sweet-smelling fillings, although lavender is wonderful for deterring moths and the aroma is hard to beat.

A *well-organized closet that makes it a pleasure to select the day's clothes*

Do you feel exhausted when you open your closet in the morning—purely at the sight of the squash and jumble of all your precious clothes crammed together? Do you end up choosing the same handful of items to wear day after day? If so, spend a rainy afternoon tackling the chaos, and make your morning choice of clothes a tranquil experience. If you have an attic or a spare-room closet, rotate your clothes and shoes according to the seasons. Hang your clothes by type (slacks together, skirts together, shirts together), and within that category by color. To avoid a jumble of shoes at the bottom of the closet, invest in a shoe rack or clear shoe boxes. Use shoe trees or tissue paper to help shoes keep their shape.

A new bag with that *lovely leather smell*

Investing in a good-quality leather bag, especially for everyday use, is money well spent. Such an accessory will make you feel elegant and in control, however chaotic your day may be. To maintain your bag's appearance, keep it free of dust; if necessary, wipe it with a slightly damp cloth and use a small amount of a purpose-made cleaner once a month. Many bags are sold with a soft cloth bag for storage; keep it for those seasons when you put your bag away. Above all, don't overfill a beloved bag with bulky objects that will ruin its shape. Every few weeks, have a thorough clear-out of old receipts, tissues, and scraps of paper that will make you feel anything less than chic.

Giving yourself a facial massage

If time and money are too short for a visit to the beauty salon, you can give your face a massage at home—it will leave the skin feeling refreshed and rejuvenated. Before you start, make sure your hands are clean.

❋ Add two drops of rose and two drops of geranium essential oils to a tablespoon of base oil—almond, grapeseed, or jojoba—and mix well.

❋ Using the fingertips of both hands, apply the oil mixture to your face in stroking movements. Start with the forehead and move out to the temples, and repeat. Move down to the nose and out to the cheeks, and repeat. From the chin, move up the jawline to the ears, and repeat.

❋ Place your middle and index fingers together between your nose and upper lip and move them in a circular motion around your mouth. Then add your ring fingers to your middle and index fingers, and begin applying gentle pressure with a circular movement around your forehead. Start in the middle of your forehead and move out toward the temples. Begin again at the nose and move out to the cheeks. Then begin again at your chin and move up the jawline to the ears.

❋ To finish, lightly tap your entire face with the index, middle, and ring fingers of both hands. Move from the center of your forehead outward, then from your nose out, from the top of your lip out, and from your chin out.

A *tidy desk adorned with a small bunch of fresh flowers*

If you think you spend far too many hours at work, you are not alone—but there are plenty of things that can be done to improve the quality of your working environment. One effective strategy is to transform your immediate surroundings from a sea of out-of-date paperwork into a calm, attractive space. Arrange all your papers in carefully labeled files and throw away things you no longer need. Find pretty containers for your desktop in which to store pens and other implements—and buy a small bunch of flowers each week. A single variety of flower in a single color is normally the best option for a work setting. You will get better value for money if you buy seasonally—for example, tulips and narcissi in the spring, roses and lilies in the summer, and chrysanthemums in the fall.

An ice-cold margarita on a hot summer's evening

2 oz. (50 ml) gold tequila
¾ oz. (20 ml) triple sec
1 oz. (25 ml) fresh lime juice
lime wheel, to garnish
salt (for the glass)*

All you need to create a margarita is good-quality tequila, lime, and orange-flavored liqueur. Add all the ingredients to a shaker filled with ice. Shake sharply and strain into a frosted, salt-rimmed margarita glass. Garnish with a lime wheel.

*To apply the salt, wipe the outside rim of the glass with lime or lemon juice, invert the glass, and dip it into a bed of salt, taking care that the salt coats only the outside of the rim.

*B*eautiful notepaper and envelopes

In these days of electronic communication—email, voicemail, and text messaging—sending or receiving a letter or invitation on good-quality stationery is a real treat.

❀ Next time a friend or relative gives you a gift or cooks you a delicious dinner, express your thanks with a handwritten note rather than a hasty email.

❀ Party invitations written, printed, or embossed on stylish thick cards and sent in matching envelopes will increase the sense of anticipation before the event and make your guests feel they have been asked to take part in a special occasion.

❀ Make the experience of letter-writing even more pleasurable by buying scented stationery, or add a few drops of essential oil to your notepaper.

*F*inding exactly the shoes you want at a bargain price—and in the right size

Retail therapy gets no better than finding your ideal pair of shoes at a knock-down price. But however beautiful the shoes may be, they must also be the right size, since ill-fitting shoes can cause health problems.

❀ The best time of day to try on shoes in a store is late afternoon, when—if you have had a normally active day—your feet will be at their widest.

❀ A well-fitting pair of shoes will allow you to move your toes around comfortably without any feeling of restriction.

❀ Wear socks or hose during the fitting session—whatever you are most likely to wear with the style of shoes you want.

❀ If shoes feel too tight when you try them on, don't buy them. They are unlikely to stretch much, especially if they are made from synthetic materials.

❀ Most people have one foot larger than the other (with the larger foot usually being on the opposite side of the body from the hand they use for writing). Always choose a pair of shoes based on the size of your larger foot.

❀ Before making a final decision, stand up in the shoes and walk around the store for a few minutes to make sure that, as well as looking great, they really are a perfect fit.

Receiving a bouquet of flowers that you hadn't expected

We all love to receive a surprise bouquet—especially if it arrives in the middle of a working day—and giving flowers as a gift needn't involve huge expense. Although many florists and supermarkets use cheap paper to wrap flowers, it doesn't take much to make even the most ordinary blooms look sensational. You can replace the florist's wrapping with generous amounts of tissue paper and shiny cellophane, and secure the paper with raffia or ribbon. Choose colors that complement the flowers and make the bow big and bold. Vibrant hot-pink paper looks funky wrapped around acid-green chrysanthemums, while paler shades emphasize the delicacy of orchids and their satiny pearls. Ordinary brown wrapping paper is neutral enough to suit most flowers, from the sculptural simplicity of a few bold stems to the most lavish bouquet.

Tea in a proper teacup

How you brew tea depends on personal taste and the specific leaves and brewing vessel you use, so experiment to discover what works best for you.

❀ For black and oolong teas, you need about one rounded teaspoon of whole leaves per cup, and slightly less for broken leaves, unless you like strong tea.

❀ For green tea and fine white teas, use about two rounded teaspoons per cup.

❀ Use freshly drawn cold water and bring it to the boil. Turn off the kettle as soon as the water boils or it will become deoxygenated and the resulting brew will be less bright in flavor.

❀ Warm the pot—or cup, if using an infuser—by swilling hot water around the inside, then pouring it away.

❀ Pour just-boiled water onto black and oolong teas. For green and white teas leave the water to cool for 2 to 3 minutes before pouring it onto the leaves.

❀ Black tea needs about 5 minutes to brew for whole leaves, 2 to 3 minutes for broken leaves. Fine Darjeelings and green tea need 2 to 3 minutes. Oolongs need about 7 minutes, and white about 10 minutes. Tea left on the leaves for too long, especially green tea, becomes astringent and bitter.

A glass of milk and a brownie

Brownies are not complicated to make—but the better the chocolate, the better they will be. The ideal texture for a brownie is just set on top, and wonderfully gooey and melting on the inside.

3 oz. (75 g) hazelnuts
10 oz. (275 g) chocolate*
1 cup (225 g) unsalted butter
3 eggs
1 cup (225 g) superfine sugar
1/3 cup (75 g) self-raising flour
2 teaspoons ground cinnamon
4 oz. (100 g) white chocolate chips

a baking tray, 7 in x 11 in (18 x 28 cm)

serves 8–12

❀ Put the hazelnuts in a dry skillet and toast over a medium heat until aromatic. Do not let them burn. Let cool, then chop coarsely.

❀ Put the chocolate and butter in a double boiler over simmering water and melt gently.

❀ Crack the eggs into a bowl, add the sugar, and beat until pale. Stir in the melted chocolate, flour, cinnamon, white chocolate chips, and chopped hazelnuts.

❀ Spoon into a greased, based-lined baking tray and bake in a preheated oven at 375°F (190°C) for 35–40 minutes, until the top sets but the mixture still feels soft underneath.

❀ Remove from the oven and let it cool in the pan. Cut into squares and serve.

*dark chocolate with at least 70 percent cocoa solids

*D*isplaying old photographs that you have come across by chance

Retrieving and displaying old family photographs can create an atmosphere of security and stability in your home, making you feel more rooted in where you belong at times of stress or uncertainty. Instead of simply framing images in the conventional way, why not create a family pinboard or hang photographs from strips of tape? You can combine them with other images that have meaning for you, such as postcards, invitation cards, tickets, or even beautifully addressed envelopes. These displays can be added to or changed.

*H*ot chocolate on a cold day

Chocolate with a hint of after-dinner mints is just the thing to send you off into a peaceful sleep or warm you up on a chilly winter's afternoon.

1 1/4 pints (600 ml) milk
4 sprigs fresh mint, lightly
* bruised to extract flavor*
2 oz. (50 g) dark chocolate,
* chopped*
sugar, to taste (optional)

serves 2

❀ Put the milk and mint sprigs in a saucepan and heat very gently until boiling. Boil for 1 minute. Remove from the heat. Discard the mint.
❀ Divide the chocolate between two mugs. Stir in the milk and continue to stir until melted.
❀ Serve the sugar separately, if using.

White hyacinths in winter

In the depths of winter the sweet but slightly spicy smell of hyacinths holds the promise of spring. You will find that the white bulbs are the most popular—and definitely the most stylish—so buy them as soon as you see them for sale early in the fall.

❀ Hyacinths are inexpensive to buy in supermarkets, and look great in bulk planted in a bowl or plastic-lined basket or box, with moss packed around the top to cover the earth.

❀ Alternatively, buy bulbs specially prepared for forcing and start them off in a cool, dark closet. Flowering should take between eight and ten weeks, so if you want flowers at Christmas plant the bulbs in September.

❀ When the shoots are at least 1½ in. (4 cm) long, move them into a cool, well-lit place for a few days before introducing them to a warmer environment.

❀ Take care not to overwater the bulbs or to expose them to too much heat immediately after they have emerged from the darkness.

❀ After flowering, you can plant the bulbs outdoors, where they should continue to flower in spring for several more years.

Throwing a dinner party at which everyone has a great time

The first secret of successful entertaining is to look relaxed and happy to see your friends when they arrive—whatever your true state of mind. There is nothing worse than being greeted by a stressed host.

❀ When you invite people to dinner, ask them if there's anything they can't eat.

❀ Keep it simple and make sure at least one course can be prepared a day in advance or on the morning of your party.

❀ If you are preparing a table plan, think it through carefully. Mix up shy and boisterous people to avoid having a lopsided meal.

❀ Set the scene with lighting. Turn off or dim ceiling lights and opt for votive or church candles or lanterns. Candlelight is always flattering and atmospheric.

❀ Tastes vary, but reckon on about 3/4 bottle of wine per person.

❀ Always offer plenty of spring water—still and sparkling.

❀ Think about balance. Serve only one cheesy dish in a meal. If you are having a cream sauce with the main course, don't serve cream or ice cream with dessert. If you had seafood for the first course, don't have fish for main, and so on.

❀ Don't start clearing up while people are obviously still enjoying themselves.

❀ Accept help gracefully—but only from friends who will genuinely assist.

The perfect, classic martini

Stirring is the authentic way to make a classic martini, but the pouring or diamond method is faster and the resultant drink stronger (less dilute).

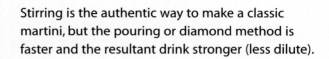

a dash of vermouth (Noilly Prat or Martini Extra Dry)
3 oz. (75 ml) freezing gin or vodka
an olive or a lemon twist, to garnish

Add the vermouth and the gin or vodka to a mixing glass filled with ice and stir. Strain into a frosted martini glass and garnish with an olive or a lemon twist.

For the coldest, purest martini, put a bottle of gin or vodka into a freezer for 6 hours. To serve, add a dash of vermouth to a chilled glass, swill it around and discard. Pour the spirit into the glass.

*W*eekend breakfast in bed

Smoked-salmon bagels with poached eggs is a light alternative to a heavy breakfast—and it's so easy to make. Treat yourself to this wonderful meal or, better still, get someone to make it for you.

2 bagels
butter, for spreading
sprigs of watercress
   or arugula
¼ lb. (100 g) smoked
   salmon
2 eggs
sea salt and freshly
   ground black pepper
fresh chives, to serve

serves 2

❋ Cut the bagels in half, toast them, then lightly spread with butter. Top with watercress or arugula, folds of salmon, and freshly ground black pepper.
❋ Crack the eggs into separate cups. Bring a large saucepan of water to a boil and, when simmering, stir the water around in one direction to create a whirlpool.
❋ Gently slip each egg into the water, return to a gentle simmer, and cover with a lid. Remove the saucepan from the heat and let stand for 6 minutes.
❋ Remove the eggs with a slotted spoon and drain on folded paper towels.
❋ Place the eggs on top of the bagels and add the chives.

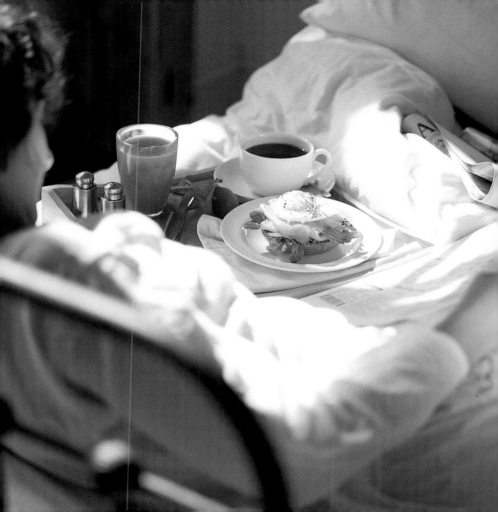

Luxurious comfort—in the shape of a wonderful couch

A really comfortable couch can transform your life—but it will always be a big investment.

❋ While wall colors and accessories such as pillows, rugs, and throws can be changed easily and cheaply, a couch needs to last at least a decade.

❋ Buy something with a strong, simple shape that will go with both antiques and modern pieces.

❋ Do your research—the price of couches is often greatly reduced in January and summer sales, but don't get carried away by the discounts.

❋ Spend plenty of time sitting on your dream couch in the store before you make the final decision. Explore the options for different levels of firmness.

❋ Try to find a couch with removable washable covers, especially if it's a pale color. You don't want to be scared of spilling something every time you sit down.

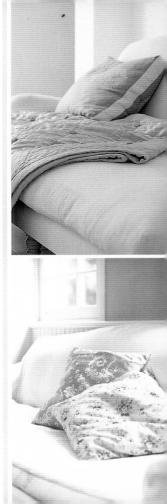

*W*atching your favorite movie with a friend and something wicked to eat

Here are ten movies guaranteed to make you feel good.

* ❋ *An Affair to Remember.*
* ❋ *When Harry Met Sally.*
* ❋ *The Big Easy.*
* ❋ *Hannah and Her Sisters.*
* ❋ *Four Weddings and a Funeral.*
* ❋ *Casablanca.*
* ❋ *It Happened One Night.*
* ❋ *Sliding Doors.*
* ❋ *Amélie.*
* ❋ *Breakfast at Tiffany's.*

Old-fashioned roses: *their power and allure*

Prized since ancient times, rose oil is still used as an ingredient in many of the most luxurious and exquisite perfumes, and in cosmetics.

❀ Rosewater makes a soothing toner, and rose oil is said to help dry, sensitive, or mature skin (including conditions such as broken capillaries and eczema).

❀ Rose oil is used by aromatherapists for its therapeutic properties.

❀ Damask, Centifolia or cabbage roses, and Gallicas are among the varieties most widely grown as commercial crops; their oil is valued for its ability to ease depression, stress, and premenstrual tension, and for its antiseptic, anti-inflammatory properties.

❀ Rose oil reputedly has aphrodisiac qualities, which explains why Cleopatra is said to have covered her palace floors in rose petals to aid in her seduction of Mark Antony.

Enjoying a glass of champagne with someone you love

Choose a light, fresh style of champagne that you can serve on its own. Typically, the predominant flavors will be fruity—citrus and apple with maybe a hint of peach and vanilla. Perfect for a romantic moment!

❀ Most inexpensive sparkling wines and non-vintage champagnes fall into the fruity category, although those labeled Blanc de Noirs may be more full-bodied.
❀ There are also certain champagne houses that are noted for making their non-vintage champagne in this style—Laurent Perrier, Perrier-Jouët, Pommery, and Tattinger, for instance—though they will become more weighty with age.
❀ Non-vintage champagne and sparkling wines made from Chardonnay alone, known as Blanc de Blancs, also tend to have a creamy vanilla edge that puts them firmly into the light-bodied camp, as do some French *crémant* wines that include a smattering of Chardonnay.
❀ Bone-dry champagnes—known as *ultra brut* or *extra brut*—that have no added sugar are always light and elegant in style.

*S*oaking in a warm tub at the end of the day

Think of your bathroom as a haven of pure relaxation—a place where you can retreat to indulge yourself and find an antidote to "stress overload."

❀ Set the scene by dimming the lights and lighting a scented candle.

❀ Add three drops each of geranium, lavender, and neroli, or two drops each of lavender, frankincense, and sandalwood essential oils to a full bathtub, step in, and immerse yourself in the fragrant warm water.

❀ Rest your neck and shoulders in the tub with a bath pillow. Lie back and imagine the waves gently lapping around your shoulders, and relax.

❀ Practice breathing deeply, close your eyes, and imagine you are at the beach or by a swimming pool—the most popular "happy" places to visualize.

❀ Soak for a full 20 minutes. As you soak, place some soothing eye pads over your lids.

*F*reshly ironed sheets

The sensation of getting into bed between clean, freshly ironed sheets is hard to beat. The finest quality cotton sheets are made of Egyptian cotton, which feels smoother and stronger because the fibers are longer. Look for as high a thread count as possible. The best is around 250 per square inch, but 200 per square inch is much more common. The closer the weave, the better the quality. Ironing sheets is a chore, so invest in fitted sheets for the mattress and fold flat sheets in half, iron, then fold completely. Always iron sheets and pillowslips when they are still damp. There are some wonderful scented linen sprays available to add fragrance to the ironing.

*R*eading in bed

Here are ten novels guaranteed to make you feel good.

❀ *I Capture the Castle* by Dodie Smith.
❀ *Miss Pettigrew Lives for A Day* by Winifred Watson.
❀ *Persuasion* by Jane Austen.
❀ *Zuleika Dobson* by Max Beerbohm.
❀ *The Priory* by Dorothy Whipple.

❀ *The Republic of Love* by Carol Shields.
❀ *Seventh Heaven* by Alice Hoffman.
❀ *The Accidental Tourist* by Anne Tyler.
❀ *Bridget Jones's Diary* by Helen Fielding.
❀ *The No.1 Ladies' Detective Agency* by Alexander McCall Smith.

*A*nd finally …
here are 14 other
little pleasures
that contribute to
the perfect day

❀ Wearing real silk underwear.

❀ Walking on dewy grass in bare feet.

❀ Waking up and realizing it's Sunday.

❀ The arrival of an unexpected check.

❀ A good gossip.

❀ Finding the perfect lipstick.

❀ Anything made of cashmere.

❀ Discovering that your next birthday falls
on a weekend.

❀ A haircut that's just what you wanted.

❀ The smell of toast at the weekend.

❀ Flirting.

❀ A long chat with an old friend.

❀ The smell of a baby's head.

❀ Discovering that you can fit into your skinny
jeans with no pain involved.

*C*redits

The publishers would like to thank
the following authors for permission to reproduce from copyright material:
Fiona Beckett, page 55; Cindy Harris, page 59; Louise Pickford, pages 34, 38;
Ben Reed, pages 24, 44; Fran Warde, pages 13, 46; Lesley Waters, page 42.

Other excerpts have been adapted from text by the following authors:
Josephine Collins, page 21; Sandra Deeble, page 42; Hattie Ellis, pages 10, 32;
Jo Glanville-Blackburn, pages 8, 56; Charlotte Packer, page 31; Antonia Swinson, page 52.

PHOTOGRAPHY CREDITS
Caroline Arber, page 4; Jan Baldwin, pages 7, 24 below; Carolyn Barber, pages
31 above, 31 below; Martin Brigdale, pages 38 above, 39; Henry Bourne, page 40;
Peter Cassidy, pages 2, 35, 55; Nicky Dowey, page 13; Dan Duchars, pages 22, 52, 63;
Chris Everard, pages 20, 21, 28, 29; Daniel Farmer, page 42; Craig Fordham, page 30;
Catherine Gratwicke, endpapers, page 19; Tom Leighton, page 38 below;
William Lingwood, pages 46–47, 48, 49; David Montgomery, pages 8, 9, 16, 56, 57, 58–59;
Debi Treloar, pages 1, 3, 10, 11, 12, 14, 15, 18, 32, 33, 34, 36, 37, 45 all, 51 above, 53, 62;
Ian Wallace, page 54; Andrew Wood, page 61;
Polly Wreford, pages 6, 17, 23, 24 above, 25, 26, 27, 43, 50, 51 below, 60.